OEDIPUS THE KING

SOPHOCLES

OEDIPUS THE KING

Translated and with an Introduction by

DAVID GRENE

THE UNIVERSITY OF CHICAGO PRESS

CHICAGO & LONDON

The University of Chicago Press, Chicago 60637
The University of Chicago Press, Ltd., London

© 2010 by The University of Chicago

Introduction © 1991 by The University of Chicago

Sophocles: Oedipus the King
© 1942 by The University of Chicago

19 18 17 16 15 14 13 12 11 10   1 2 3 4 5

ISBN-13: 978-0-226-76868-7 (paper)
ISBN-10: 0-226-76868-6 (paper)

Library of Congress Cataloging-in-Publication Data

Sophocles.
  [Oedipus Rex. English]
  Oedipus the King / Sophocles ; translated and with an introduction by
David Grene.
       p. cm.
  Contains Grene's 1942 translation of Oedipus Rex; also includes
Grene's 1991 introduction to Sophocles I, entitled The Theban plays by
Sophocles.
  ISBN-13: 978-0-226-76868-7 (pbk. : alk. paper)
  ISBN-10: 0-226-76868-6 (pbk. : alk. paper)
  I. Grene, David. II. Sophocles. Sophocles I. III. Title. IV. Title:
Theban plays by Sophocles.
  PA4414.O7G74 2010
  882'.01—dc22

                         2009038278

♾ The paper used in this publication meets the minimum requirements of the American
National Standard for Information Sciences—Permanence of Paper for Printed Library
Materials, ANSI Z39.48 1992.

INTRODUCTION

"The Theban Plays" by Sophocles

T HIS series of plays, *Oedipus the King, Oedipus at Colonus,* and *Antigone,* was written over a wide interval of years. The dating is only approximate, for reliable evidence is lacking; but the *Antigone* was produced in 441 B.C. when Sophocles was probably fifty-four, and *Oedipus the King* some fourteen or fifteen years later. *Oedipus at Colonus* was apparently produced the year after its author's death at the age of ninety in 405 B.C. Thus, although the three plays are concerned with the same legend, they were not conceived and executed at the same time and with a single purpose, as is the case with Aeschylus' *Oresteia*. We can here see how a story teased the imagination of Sophocles until it found its final expression. We can see the degrees of variation in treatment he gave the myth each time he handled it. And perhaps we can come to some notion of what the myths meant to Sophocles as raw material for the theater.

The internal dramatic dates of the three plays do not agree with the order of their composition. As far as the legend is concerned, the story runs in sequence: *Oedipus the King, Oedipus at Colonus, Antigone*. But Sophocles wrote them in the order: *Antigone, Oedipus the King, Oedipus at Colonus*. In view of this and the long interval between the composition of the individual plays, we would expect some inconsistencies between the three versions. And there are fairly serious inconsistencies—in facts, for instance. At the conclusion of *Oedipus the King,* Creon is in undisputed authority after the removal of Oedipus. Though he appeals to him to look after his daughters, Oedipus refrains from asking Creon to do anything for his sons, who, he says, will be all right on their own (*OK* 1460). It is Creon who will succeed Oedipus in Thebes, and there is no question of any legitimate claim of Oedipus' descendants (*OK* 1418). But in *Antigone,* Creon tells the chorus that he has favorably observed their loyalty first to Oedipus and then to his sons, and so has hope of their devotion to himself. In *Oedipus at Colonus*—the last of the three plays he wrote—Sophocles makes one of his very few clumsy efforts to patch the discrepancies together. In *Oedipus at Colonus* (ll. 367 ff.), Ismene says that *at first* the two sons were willing to leave the throne to Creon in view of their fatal family heritage, but after a while they decided to take over the monarchy and the quarrel was only between themselves as to who should succeed. At this point Creon has vanished out of the picture altogether! Again, the responsibility for the decision to expel Oedipus from Thebes and keep him out rests, in *Oedipus the King,* entirely with Creon, who announces that he will consult Apollo in the matter. In *Oedipus at Colonus* his sons' guilt in condemning their father to exile is one of the bitterest counts in Oedipus' indictment of them (*OC* 1360 ff.). These are important differences. We do not know anything really certain about the manner of publication of the plays after their production. We know even less about Sophocles' treatment of his own scripts. Maybe he simply did not bother to keep them after he saw them as far as the stage, though that seems unlikely. Or it is possible and likelier that Sophocles, as he wrote the last play in extreme old age and in what seems to be the characteristic self-absorption of the last years of his life, cared little about whether *Oedipus at Colonus* exactly tallied, in its presentation, with the stories he had written thirty-seven and twenty-two years earlier.

Let us for the moment disregard the details of the story and concentrate on what would seem to be the central theme of the first two plays in order of composition. And here we find something very curious. Most critics have felt the significance of the *Antigone* to lie in the opposition of Creon and Antigone and all that this opposition represents. It is thus a play about something quite different from *Oedipus the King.* And yet what a remarkable similarity there is in the dilemma of Creon in *Antigone* and Oedipus himself in the first Oedipus play. In both of them a king has taken a decision which is disobeyed or questioned by his subjects. In both, the ruler misconstrues the role of the rebel and his own as a sovereign. In both, he has a crucial encounter with the priest Teiresias, who warns him that the forces of religion are against him. In both, he charges that the priest has been suborned. There the resemblance ends; for, after abusing the old prophet, Creon is overcome with fear of his authority and, too late, tries to undo his mistake. In *Oedipus the King* the king defies all assaults upon his decision until the deadly self-knowledge which starts to work in him has accomplished its course and he is convicted out of his own mouth.

Usually, as we know, the *Antigone* is interpreted entirely as the conflict between Creon and Antigone. It has often been regarded as the classical statement of the struggle between the law of the individual conscience and the central power of the state. Unquestionably, these issues are inherent in the play. Unquestionably, even, Sophocles would understand the modern way of seeing his play, for the issue of the opposition of the individual and the state was sufficiently present to his mind to make this significant for him. But can the parallelism between the position of Oedipus in the one play and Creon in the other be quite irrelevant to the interpretation of the two? And is it not very striking that such a large share of the *Antigone* should be devoted to the conclusion of the conflict, as far as Creon is concerned, and to the destruction of his human happiness?

What I would suggest is this: that Sophocles had at the time of writing the first play (in 442 B.C.) a theme in mind which centered in the Theban trilogy. One might express it by saying that it is the story of a ruler who makes a mistaken decision, though in good faith, and who then finds himself opposed in a fashion which he misunderstands and which induces him to persist in his mistake. This story is later on going to be that of a man who breaks divine law without realizing that he is doing so, and whose destruction is then brought about by the voice of the divine law in society. Between the *Antigone* and *Oedipus the King,* the theme has developed further, for in the latter play Sophocles is showing how the ruler who breaks the divine law may, for all he can see and understand, be entirely innocent, but nonetheless his guilt is an objective fact. In the third play, *Oedipus at Colonus,* this issue reaches its final statement. The old Oedipus is admittedly a kind of monster. Wherever he comes, people shrink from him. Yet his guilt carries with it some sort of innocence on which God will set his seal. For the old man is both cursed and blessed. The god gives him an extraordinary end, and the last place of his mortal habitation is blessed forever.

What this interpretation would mean, if correct, is that Sophocles started to write about the Theban legend, the story of Oedipus and his children, without having fully understood what he wanted to say about it. He may have been, and probably was, drawn, unknown to himself, to the dramatization of this particular legend because in it lay the material of the greatest theme of his later artistic life. But first he tried his hand at it in the opposition of Creon and Antigone. However, even while he did this, the character of Creon and his role in the play were shaping what was to be the decisive turn in the story he was going to write—the Oedipus saga.

Thus there is a certain elasticity in the entire treatment of myth. The author will accent a certain character at one time to suit a play and change the accent to suit another. Or he may even discover the same theme in a different myth. This is suggested by a short comparison of the *Philoctetes* and *Oedipus at Colonus,* both written in the last few years of Sophocles' life. The figure of Philoctetes, though occurring in a totally different legend from Oedipus, is a twin child with Oedipus in Sophocles' dramatic imagination. In both these plays, the *Philoctetes* and *Oedipus at Colonus,* the hero is a man whose value is inextricably coupled with his offensive quality. Philoctetes is the archer whose bow will overcome Troy. He is also the creature whose stinking infested wound moves everyone to disgust who has to do with him. Oedipus is accursed in the sight of all men; he had committed the two crimes, parricide and incest, which rendered him an outcast in any human society. But he is also the one to whom, at his end, God will give the marks of his favor, and the place where he is last seen on earth will be lucky and blessed. This combination of the evil and the good is too marked, in these two plays, to be accidental. It is surely the idea which inspired the old Sophocles for his two last plays. There is, however, an important further development of the theme in the *Oedipus at Colonus.* For there in Oedipus' mind the rational innocence—the fact that he had committed the offenses unknowingly—is, for him at least, important in God's final justification of him. Sophocles is declaring that the sin of Oedipus is real; that the consequences in the form of the loneliness, neglect, and suffering of the years of wandering are inevitable; but that the will and the consciousness are also some measure of man's sin—and when the sinner sinned necessarily and unwittingly, his suffering can be compensation enough for his guilt. He may at the end be blessed and a blessing. This is not the same doctrine as that of Aeschylus, when he asserts that through suffering comes wisdom. Nor is it the Christian doctrine of a man purified by suffering as by fire. Oedipus in his contact with Creon, in his interview with Polyneices shows himself as bitter, sudden in anger, and implacable as ever. He is indeed a monstrous old man. But at the last, he is, in a measure, *vindicated*. Yet in *Philoctetes* the theme of the union of the offensive and the beneficial, which in *Oedipus at Colonus* becomes the curse and the blessing, is seen without the addition of conscious innocence and unconscious guilt. Can we say that Sophocles finally felt that the consciousness of innocence in Oedipus is the balancing factor in the story? That in this sense *Oedipus at Colonus* is the further step beyond *Philoctetes* in the clarification of the dramatic subject which occupied the very old author? Or that the consciousness of innocence when linked with objective guilt is only the human shield against the cruelty of the irrational—that Oedipus is meaningful in his combination of guilt and innocence as a manifestation of God and of destiny and that his explanation of his conscious innocence is only the poor human inadequate explanation? Everyone will answer this according to his own choice. But, clearly, the theme of Philoctetes and the theme of the old Oedipus are connected.

If an analysis such as this has importance, it is to show the relation of Sophocles to the raw material of his plays—the myth. It is to show the maturing of a theme in Sophocles' mind and his successive treatments of it in the same and different legends. In the Oedipus story it is a certain fundamental situation which becomes significant for Sophocles, and the characters are altered to suit the story. Creon in the first, Oedipus in the second, are examples of the same sort of dilemma, even though the dilemma of Creon in the *Antigone* is incidental to the main emphasis of the play, which is on Antigone. But the dilemma was to be much more fruitful for Sophocles as a writer and thinker than the plain issue between Antigone and Creon. The dilemma resolves itself in the last play at the end of Sophocles' life into the dramatic statement of a principle, of the union of the blessed and the cursed, of the just and the unjust, and sometimes (not always) of the consciously innocent and the unconsciously guilty. The fact that Sophocles could in two successive treatments of the play fifteen years apart switch the parts of Creon and Oedipus indicates that neither the moral color of the characters nor even their identity was absolutely fixed in his mind. The same conclusion is borne out by the great similarity between the *Philoctetes* and the *Oedipus at Colonus.* Sophocles in his last days was incessantly thinking of the man who is blessed and cursed. For the theater he became once the lame castaway Philoctetes, who yet, in virtue of his archery, is to be the conqueror of Troy; in the next play he is Oedipus, who sinned against the order of human society but is still to be the blessing of Athens and the patron saint of Colonus. It is the theme and not the man that matters. Consequently, it is the kernel of the legend, as he saw it for the moment, that is sacred for Sophocles, not the identification of all the characters in a certain relation to one another. True, he has treated the Oedipus story three times in his life, which means that the Oedipus story had a certain fascination for him—that somehow hidden in it he knew there was what he wanted to say. But he did not have to think of the whole story and the interdependence of its characters when he made his changes each time. One stage of the theme borne by the hero is given to a character in a totally different myth. The sequence is Creon, Oedipus, Philoctetes, Oedipus. It may seem absurd to link Creon, the obvious form of tyrant (as conceived by the Athenians), and Philoctetes. But it is the progression we should notice. The tyrant who with true and good intentions orders what is wrong, morally and religiously, is crudely represented in Creon; he is much more subtly represented in Oedipus himself in the next play. But the similarity of the situation and the nature of the opposition to him proves how generically the character is conceived. You can switch the labels, and Creon becomes Oedipus. But if the character is generic, the situation is deepening. We are beginning to understand *why* a certain sort of tyrant may be a tyrant and in a shadowy way how conscious and unconscious guilt are related. In the *Philoctetes* and *Oedipus at Colonus* the situation is being seen in its last stages. We are no longer concerned with how Philoctetes came to sin or how Oedipus is the author of his own ruin. But only how does it feel to be an object both of disgust and of fear to your fellows, while you yourself are simultaneously aware of the injustice of your treatment and at last, in *Oedipus at Colonus,* of the objective proofs of God's favor.

For Sophocles the myth was the treatment of the generic aspect of human dilemmas. What he made of the myth in his plays was neither history nor the kind of dramatic creation represented by *Hamlet* or *Macbeth*. Not history, for in no sense is the uniqueness of the event or the uniqueness of the character important; not drama in the Shakespearean sense, because Sophocles' figures do not have, as Shakespeare's do, the timeless and complete reality in themselves. Behind the figure of Oedipus or Creon stands the tyrant of the legend; and behind the tyrant of the legend, the meaning of all despotic authority. Behind the old Oedipus is the beggar and wanderer of the legend, and behind him the mysterious human combination of opposites—opposites in meaning and in fact. And so the character may fluctuate or the names may vary. It is the theme, the generic side of tragedy, which is important; it is there that the emphasis of the play rests.

FURTHER INTRODUCTORY NOTE, 1991

My version of *Oedipus the King* was written fifty years ago. Of the two other translations which also formerly appeared in this volume, Robert Fitzgerald's *Oedipus at Colonus* is of almost the same vintage and Elizabeth Wyckoff's *Antigone* is more than thirty years old. As the remaining editor of *The Complete Greek*

Tragedies I have been looking through the series, at the suggestion of the Press, and have been making some alterations. Perhaps some of my criticisms may have been misplaced, but certain features of these translations by Wyckoff and Fitzgerald seemed unsatisfactory. Besides, despite the small inconsistencies in the story of the three plays, which I mentioned earlier, there is certainly a unity of tone and style in these Theban plays that greatly favors the same translator for all of them. So I have translated the *Antigone* and the *Oedipus at Colonus* and have substituted them for the previous renderings of Wyckoff and Fitzgerald.

Though the numbered lines of my *Oedipus the King* appear to match fairly thoroughly those of the Greek text, I have not been so successful with the combination of the Greek and the English in these last two plays. Often I have needed more space than the limitation of a line would allow. More commonly I have written two or more short lines for one of the Greek in the interest of vividness or other dramatic reasons. This has caused a confusion that I had not anticipated, and a lot of complaints. So from this reprint on, the numbering in the margins of these versions of the *Antigone* and *Oedipus at Colonnus* has been changed to correspond to that of the Greek text. With the anchor of the Greek lines, it is comparatively simple for the reader to notice where he or she is in the text, and notice (I hope without resentment) the purely formal difference of the number of lines rendering it.

Some years ago the Court Theatre asked Wendy Doniger and me to do a new prose version of the *Antigone* for their repertory company. We worked in very close collaboration with the actors. Because the Court Theatre rendering was in prose, and all the other plays in the series of *The Complete Greek Tragedies* were overwhelmingly in verse, I decided to write the *Antigone* and *Oedipus at Colonnus* in my new translation in verse. But I owe a great deal to the earlier prose version of the *Antigone*, which I gladly acknowledge, and to Wendy Doniger's participation in it.

UNIVERSITY OF CHICAGO   DAVID GRENE

OEDIPUS THE KING

CHARACTERS

Oedipus, King of Thebes

Jocasta, His Wife

Creon, His Brother-in-Law

Teiresias, an Old Blind Prophet

A Priest

First Messenger

Second Messenger

A Herdsman

A Chorus of Old Men of Thebes

OEDIPUS THE KING

SCENE: *In front of the palace of Oedipus at Thebes. To the right of the stage near the altar stands the Priest with a crowd of children. Oedipus emerges from the central door.*

Oedipus

Children, young sons and daughters of old Cadmus,
why do you sit here with your suppliant crowns?
The town is heavy with a mingled burden
of sounds and smells, of groans and hymns and incense;   5
I did not think it fit that I should hear
of this from messengers but came myself,—
I Oedipus whom all men call the Great.

(*He turns to the Priest.*)

You're old and they are young; come, speak for them.
What do you fear or want, that you sit here   10
suppliant? Indeed I'm willing to give all
that you may need; I would be very hard
should I not pity suppliants like these.

Priest

O ruler of my country, Oedipus,
you see our company around the altar;   15
you see our ages; some of us, like these,
who cannot yet fly far, and some of us
heavy with age; these children are the chosen
among the young, and I the priest of Zeus.
Within the market place sit others crowned   20
with suppliant garlands, at the double shrine
of Pallas and the temple where Ismenus
gives oracles by fire. King, you yourself
have seen our city reeling like a wreck
already; it can scarcely lift its prow
out of the depths, out of the bloody surf.

A blight is on the fruitful plants of the earth,   25
A blight is on the cattle in the fields,
a blight is on our women that no children
are born to them; a God that carries fire,
a deadly pestilence, is on our town,
strikes us and spares not, and the house of Cadmus
is emptied of its people while black Death
grows rich in groaning and in lamentation.   30
We have not come as suppliants to this altar
because we thought of you as of a God,
but rather judging you the first of men
in all the chances of this life and when
we mortals have to do with more than man.
You came and by your coming saved our city,   35
freed us from tribute which we paid of old
to the Sphinx, cruel singer. This you did
in virtue of no knowledge we could give you,
in virtue of no teaching; it was God
that aided you, men say, and you are held
with God's assistance to have saved our lives.
Now Oedipus, Greatest in all men's eyes,   40
here falling at your feet we all entreat you,
find us some strength for rescue.
Perhaps you'll hear a wise word from some God,
perhaps you will learn something from a man
(for I have seen that for the skilled of practice
the outcome of their counsels live the most).   45
Noblest of men, go, and raise up our city,
go,—and give heed. For now this land of ours
calls you its savior since you saved it once.
So, let us never speak about your reign
as of a time when first our feet were set
secure on high, but later fell to ruin.   50
Raise up our city, save it and raise it up.
Once you have brought us luck with happy omen;
be no less now in fortune.

If you will rule this land, as now you rule it,
better to rule it full of men than empty.   55
For neither tower nor ship is anything
when empty, and none live in it together.

Oedipus

I pity you, children. You have come full of longing,
but I have known the story before you told it
only too well. I know you are all sick,
yet there is not one of you, sick though you are,   60
that is as sick as I myself.
Your several sorrows each have single scope
and touch but one of you. My spirit groans
for city and myself and you at once.
You have not roused me like a man from sleep;   65
know that I have given many tears to this,
gone many ways wandering in thought,
but as I thought I found only one remedy
and that I took. I sent Menoeceus' son
Creon, Jocasta's brother, to Apollo,   70
to his Pythian temple,
that he might learn there by what act or word
I could save this city. As I count the days,
it vexes me what ails him; he is gone
far longer than he needed for the journey.   75
But when he comes, then, may I prove a villain,
if I shall not do all the God commands.

Priest

Thanks for your gracious words. Your servants here
signal that Creon is this moment coming.

Oedipus

His face is bright. O holy Lord Apollo,   80
grant that his news too may be bright for us
and bring us safety.

Priest

    It is happy news,
    I think, for else his head would not be crowned
    with sprigs of fruitful laurel.

Oedipus

                We will know soon,
    he's within hail. Lord Creon, my good brother,   85
    what is the word you bring us from the God?

                        (Creon enters.)

Creon

    A good word,—for things hard to bear themselves
    if in the final issue all is well
    I count complete good fortune.

Oedipus

                What do you mean?
    What you have said so far
    leaves me uncertain whether to trust or fear.   90

Creon

    If you will hear my news before these others
    I am ready to speak, or else to go within.

Oedipus

    Speak it to all;
    the grief I bear, I bear it more for these
    than for my own heart.

Creon

                I will tell you, then,   95
    what I heard from the God.
    King Phoebus in plain words commanded us
    to drive out a pollution from our land,
    pollution grown ingrained within the land;
    drive it out, said the God, not cherish it,
    till it's past cure.

Oedipus

              What is the rite
    of purification? How shall it be done?

Creon

By banishing a man, or expiation   100
of blood by blood, since it is murder guilt
which holds our city in this destroying storm.

Oedipus

Who is this man whose fate the God pronounces?

Creon

My Lord, before you piloted the state
we had a king called Laius.

Oedipus

I know of him by hearsay. I have not seen him.   105

Creon

The God commanded clearly: let some one
punish with force this dead man's murderers.

Oedipus

Where are they in the world? Where would a trace
of this old crime be found? It would be hard
to guess where.

Creon

                         The clue is in this land;   110
that which is sought is found;
the unheeded thing escapes:
so said the God.

Oedipus

                         Was it at home,
or in the country that death came upon him,
or in another country travelling?

Creon

He went, he said himself, upon an embassy,
but never returned when he set out from home.   115

Oedipus

Was there no messenger, no fellow traveller
who knew what happened? Such a one might tell
something of use.

Creon

    They were all killed save one. He fled in terror
    and he could tell us nothing in clear terms
    of what he knew, nothing, but one thing only.

Oedipus

    What was it?   120
    If we could even find a slim beginning
    in which to hope, we might discover much.

Creon

    This man said that the robbers they encountered
    were many and the hands that did the murder
    were many; it was no man's single power.

Oedipus

    How could a robber dare a deed like this
    were he not helped with money from the city,
    money and treachery?   125

Creon

                             That indeed was thought.
    But Laius was dead and in our trouble
    there was none to help.

Oedipus

    What trouble was so great to hinder you
    inquiring out the murder of your king?

Creon

    The riddling Sphinx induced us to neglect   130
    mysterious crimes and rather seek solution
    of troubles at our feet.

Oedipus

    I will bring this to light again. King Phoebus
    fittingly took this care about the dead,
    and you too fittingly.
    And justly you will see in me an ally,   135
    a champion of my country and the God.
    For when I drive pollution from the land

I will not serve a distant friend's advantage,
but act in my own interest. Whoever
he was that killed the king may readily
wish to dispatch me with his murderous hand;   140
so helping the dead king I help myself.

Come, children, take your suppliant boughs and go;
up from the altars now. Call the assembly
and let it meet upon the understanding
that I'll do everything. God will decide   145
whether we prosper or remain in sorrow.

Priest

Rise, children—it was this we came to seek,
which of himself the king now offers us.
May Phoebus who gave us the oracle
come to our rescue and stay the plague.   150

(*Exeunt all but the Chorus.*)

Chorus

Strophe

What is the sweet spoken word of God from the shrine of Pytho
    rich in gold
that has come to glorious Thebes?
I am stretched on the rack of doubt, and terror and trembling
    hold
my heart, O Delian Healer, and I worship full of fears
for what doom you will bring to pass, new or renewed in the   155
    revolving years.
Speak to me, immortal voice,
child of golden Hope.

Antistrophe

First I call on you, Athene, deathless daughter of Zeus,
and Artemis, Earth Upholder,   160
who sits in the midst of the market place in the throne which
    men call Fame,
and Phoebus, the Far Shooter, three averters of Fate,

come to us now, if ever before, when ruin rushed upon the state,   165
you drove destruction's flame away
out of our land.

Strophe

Our sorrows defy number;
all the ship's timbers are rotten;
taking of thought is no spear for the driving away of the plague.   170
There are no growing children in this famous land;
there are no women bearing the pangs of childbirth.
You may see them one with another, like birds swift on the
    wing,   175
quicker than fire unmastered,
speeding away to the coast of the Western God.

Antistrophe

In the unnumbered deaths
of its people the city dies;
those children that are born lie dead on the naked earth
unpitied, spreading contagion of death; and grey haired mothers
    and wives
everywhere stand at the altar's edge, suppliant, moaning;   182-85
the hymn to the healing God rings out but with it the wailing
    voices are blended.
From these our sufferings grant us, O golden Daughter of Zeus,
glad-faced deliverance.

Strophe

There is no clash of brazen shields but our fight is with the War
    God,
a War God ringed with the cries of men, a savage God who burns   191
    us;
grant that he turn in racing course backwards out of our coun-
    try's bounds
to the great palace of Amphitrite or where the waves of the   195
    Thracian sea
deny the stranger safe anchorage.
Whatsoever escapes the night

at last the light of day revisits;
so smite the War God, Father Zeus,
beneath your thunderbolt,
for you are the Lord of the lightning, the lightning that
    carries fire.   200

   Antistrophe
   And your unconquered arrow shafts, winged by the golden
   corded bow,
Lycean King, I beg to be at our side for help;   205
and the gleaming torches of Artemis with which she scours the
    Lycean hills,
and I call on the God with the turban of gold, who gave his name
    to this country of ours,   210
the Bacchic God with the wind flushed face,
Evian One, who travel
with the Maenad company,
combat the God that burns us
with your torch of pine;
for the God that is our enemy is a God unhonoured among the   215
    Gods.
                                  (Oedipus returns.)

Oedipus
   For what you ask me—if you will hear my words,
   and hearing welcome them and fight the plague,
   you will find strength and lightening of your load.

   Hark to me; what I say to you, I say
   as one that is a stranger to the story
   as stranger to the deed. For I would not   220
   be far upon the track if I alone
   were tracing it without a clue. But now,
   since after all was finished, I became
   a citizen among you, citizens—
   now I proclaim to all the men of Thebes:
   who so among you knows the murderer   225
   by whose hand Laius, son of Labdacus,

died—I command him to tell everything
to me,—yes, though he fears himself to take the blame
on his own head; for bitter punishment
he shall have none, but leave this land unharmed.
Or if he knows the murderer, another,   230
a foreigner, still let him speak the truth.
For I will pay him and be grateful, too.
But if you shall keep silence, if perhaps
some one of you, to shield a guilty friend,
or for his own sake shall reject my words—
hear what I shall do then: 235
I forbid that man, whoever he be, my land,
my land where I hold sovereignty and throne;
and I forbid any to welcome him
or cry him greeting or make him a sharer   240
in sacrifice or offering to the Gods,
or give him water for his hands to wash.
I command all to drive him from their homes,
since he is our pollution, as the oracle
of Pytho's God proclaimed him now to me.
So I stand forth a champion of the God
and of the man who died.   245
Upon the murderer I invoke this curse—
whether he is one man and all unknown,
or one of many—may he wear out his life
in misery to miserable doom!
If with my knowledge he lives at my hearth   250
I pray that I myself may feel my curse.
On you I lay my charge to fulfill all this
for me, for the God, and for this land of ours
destroyed and blighted, by the God forsaken.

Even were this no matter of God's ordinance   255
it would not fit you so to leave it lie,
unpurified, since a good man is dead
and one that was a king. Search it out.

Since I am now the holder of his office,
and have his bed and wife that once was his,   260
and had his line not been unfortunate
we would have common children—(fortune leaped
upon his head)—because of all these things,
I fight in his defence as for my father,
and I shall try all means to take the murderer   265
of Laius the son of Labdacus
the son of Polydorus and before him
of Cadmus and before him of Agenor.
Those who do not obey me, may the Gods
grant no crops springing from the ground they plough   270
nor children to their women! May a fate
like this, or one still worse than this consume them!
For you whom these words please, the other Thebans,
may Justice as your ally and all the Gods
live with you, blessing you now and for ever!   275

Chorus

As you have held me to my oath, I speak:
I neither killed the king nor can declare
the killer; but since Phoebus set the quest
it is his part to tell who the man is.

Oedipus

Right; but to put compulsion on the Gods   280
against their will—no man can do that.

Chorus

May I then say what I think second best?

Oedipus

If there's a third best, too, spare not to tell it.

Chorus

I know that what the Lord Teiresias
sees, is most often what the Lord Apollo   285
sees. If you should inquire of this from him
you might find out most clearly.

Oedipus

    Even in this my actions have not been sluggard.
    On Creon's word I have sent two messengers
    and why the prophet is not here already
    I have been wondering.

Chorus

                        His skill apart   290
    there is besides only an old faint story.

Oedipus

    What is it?
    I look at every story.

Chorus

                        It was said
    that he was killed by certain wayfarers.

Oedipus

    I heard that, too, but no one saw the killer.

Chorus

    Yet if he has a share of fear at all,
    his courage will not stand firm, hearing your curse.   295

Oedipus

    The man who in the doing did not shrink
    will fear no word.

Chorus

                    Here comes his prosecutor:
    led by your men the godly prophet comes
    in whom alone of mankind truth is native.

                      (Enter Teiresias, led by a little boy.)

Oedipus

    Teiresias, you are versed in everything,   300
    things teachable and things not to be spoken,
    things of the heaven and earth-creeping things.
    You have no eyes but in your mind you know
    with what a plague our city is afflicted.
    My lord, in you alone we find a champion,

in you alone one that can rescue us.
Perhaps you have not heard the messengers, 305
but Phoebus sent in answer to our sending
an oracle declaring that our freedom
from this disease would only come when we
should learn the names of those who killed King Laius,
and kill them or expel from our country.
Do not begrudge us oracles from birds, 310
or any other way of prophecy
within your skill; save yourself and the city,
save me; redeem the debt of our pollution
that lies on us because of this dead man.
We are in your hands; pains are most nobly taken
to help another when you have means and power. 315

Teiresias

Alas, how terrible is wisdom when
it brings no profit to the man that's wise!
This I knew well, but had forgotten it,
else I would not have come here.

Oedipus

What is this?
How sad you are now you have come!

Teiresias

Let me
go home. It will be easiest for us both 320
to bear our several destinies to the end
if you will follow my advice.

Oedipus

You'd rob us
of this your gift of prophecy? You talk
as one who had no care for law nor love
for Thebes who reared you.

Teiresias

Yes, but I see that even your own words
miss the mark; therefore I must fear for mine. 325

Oedipus

For God's sake if you know of anything,
do not turn from us; all of us kneel to you,
all of us here, your suppliants.

Teiresias

All of you here know nothing. I will not
bring to the light of day my troubles, mine—
rather than call them yours.

Oedipus

                    What do you mean?
You know of something but refuse to speak.   330
Would you betray us and destroy the city?

Teiresias

I will not bring this pain upon us both,
neither on you nor on myself. Why is it
you question me and waste your labour? I
will tell you nothing.

Oedipus

You would provoke a stone! Tell us, you villain,   335
tell us, and do not stand there quietly
unmoved and balking at the issue.

Teiresias

You blame my temper but you do not see
your own that lives within you; it is me
you chide.

Oedipus

Who would not feel his temper rise
at words like these with which you shame our city?   340

Teiresias

Of themselves things will come, although I hide them
and breathe no word of them.

Oedipus

                    Since they will come
tell them to me.

Teiresias

                I will say nothing further.
Against this answer let your temper rage
as wildly as you will.

Oedipus

                Indeed I am   345
so angry I shall not hold back a jot
of what I think. For I would have you know
I think you were complotter of the deed
and doer of the deed save in so far
as for the actual killing. Had you had eyes
I would have said alone you murdered him.

Teiresias

  Yes? Then I warn you faithfully to keep   350
the letter of your proclamation and
from this day forth to speak no word of greeting
to these nor me; you are the land's pollution.

Oedipus

  How shamelessly you started up this taunt!
  How do you think you will escape?   355

Teiresias

                I have.
I have escaped; the truth is what I cherish
and that's my strength.

Oedipus

              And who has taught you truth?
Not your profession surely!

Teiresias

             You have taught me,
for you have made me speak against my will.

Oedipus

  Speak what? Tell me again that I may learn it better.

Teiresias

  Did you not understand before or would you
  provoke me into speaking?   360

Oedipus

I did not grasp it,
not so to call it known. Say it again.

Teiresias

I say you are the murderer of the king
whose murderer you seek.

Oedipus

Not twice you shall
say calumnies like this and stay unpunished.

Teiresias

Shall I say more to tempt your anger more?

Oedipus

As much as you desire; it will be said   365
in vain.

Teiresias

I say that with those you love best
you live in foulest shame unconsciously
and do not see where you are in calamity.

Oedipus

Do you imagine you can always talk
like this, and live to laugh at it hereafter?

Teiresias

Yes, if the truth has anything of strength.

Oedipus

It has, but not for you; it has no strength   370
for you because you are blind in mind and ears
as well as in your eyes.

Teiresias

You are a poor wretch
to taunt me with the very insults which
every one soon will heap upon yourself.

Oedipus

Your life is one long night so that you cannot
hurt me or any other who sees the light.   375

Teiresias

    It is not fate that I should be your ruin,
    Apollo is enough; it is his care
    to work this out.

Oedipus

                    Was this your own design
    or Creon's?

Teiresias

                 Creon is no hurt to you,
    but you are to yourself.

Oedipus

    Wealth, sovereignty and skill outmatching skill   380
    for the contrivance of an envied life!
    Great store of jealousy fill your treasury chests,
    if my friend Creon, friend from the first and loyal,   385
    thus secretly attacks me, secretly
    desires to drive me out and secretly
    suborns this juggling, trick devising quack,
    this wily beggar who has only eyes
    for his own gains, but blindness in his skill.
    For, tell me, where have you seen clear, Teiresias,   390
    with your prophetic eyes? When the dark singer,
    the sphinx, was in your country, did you speak
    word of deliverance to its citizens?
    And yet the riddle's answer was not the province
    of a chance comer. It was a prophet's task
    and plainly you had no such gift of prophecy   395
    from birds nor otherwise from any God
    to glean a word of knowledge. But I came,
    Oedipus, who knew nothing, and I stopped her.
    I solved the riddle by my wit alone.
    Mine was no knowledge got from birds. And now
    you would expel me,
    because you think that you will find a place   400
    by Creon's throne. I think you will be sorry,

both you and your accomplice, for your plot
to drive me out. And did I not regard you
as an old man, some suffering would have taught you
that what was in your heart was treason.

Chorus

We look at this man's words and yours, my king,
and we find both have spoken them in anger.   405
We need no angry words but only thought
how we may best hit the God's meaning for us.

Teiresias

If you are king, at least I have the right
no less to speak in my defence against you.
Of that much I am master. I am no slave   410
of yours, but Loxias', and so I shall not
enroll myself with Creon for my patron.
Since you have taunted me with being blind,
here is my word for you.
You have your eyes but see not where you are
in sin, nor where you live, nor whom you live with.
Do you know who your parents are? Unknowing   415
you are an enemy to kith and kin
in death, beneath the earth, and in this life.
A deadly footed, double striking curse,
from father and mother both, shall drive you forth
out of this land, with darkness on your eyes,
that now have such straight vision. Shall there be
a place will not be harbour to your cries,   420
a corner of Cithaeron will not ring
in echo to your cries, soon, soon,—
when you shall learn the secret of your marriage,
which steered you to a haven in this house,—
haven no haven, after lucky voyage?
And of the multitude of other evils
establishing a grim equality
between you and your children, you know nothing.   425

So, muddy with contempt my words and Creon's!
Misery shall grind no man as it will you.

Oedipus

Is it endurable that I should hear
such words from him? Go and a curse go with you!   430
Quick, home with you! Out of my house at once!

Teiresias

I would not have come either had you not called me.

Oedipus

I did not know then you would talk like a fool—
or it would have been long before I called you.

Teiresias

I am a fool then, as it seems to you—   435
but to the parents who have bred you, wise.

Oedipus

What parents? Stop! Who are they of all the world?

Teiresias

This day will show your birth and will destroy you.

Oedipus

How needlessly your riddles darken everything.

Teiresias

But it's in riddle answering you are strongest.   440

Oedipus

Yes. Taunt me where you will find me great.

Teiresias

It is this very luck that has destroyed you.

Oedipus

I do not care, if it has saved this city.

Teiresias

Well, I will go. Come, boy, lead me away.

Oedipus

Yes, lead him off. So long as you are here,   445

you'll be a stumbling block and a vexation;
once gone, you will not trouble me again.

Teiresias

                 I have said
what I came here to say not fearing your
countenance: there is no way you can hurt me.
I tell you, king, this man, this murderer
(whom you have long declared you are in search of,
indicting him in threatening proclamation   450
as murderer of Laius)—he is here.
In name he is a stranger among citizens
but soon he will be shown to be a citizen
true native Theban, and he'll have no joy
of the discovery: blindness for sight
and beggary for riches his exchange,   455
he shall go journeying to a foreign country
tapping his way before him with a stick.
He shall be proved father and brother both
to his own children in his house; to her
that gave him birth, a son and husband both;
a fellow sower in his father's bed
with that same father that he murdered.
Go within, reckon that out, and if you find me   460
mistaken, say I have no skill in prophecy.

                  (Exeunt separately Teiresias and Oedipus.)

Chorus

    Strophe
Who is the man proclaimed
by Delphi's prophetic rock
as the bloody handed murderer,   465
the doer of deeds that none dare name?
Now is the time for him to run
with a stronger foot
than Pegasus
for the child of Zeus leaps in arms upon him   470
with fire and the lightning bolt,

and terribly close on his heels
are the Fates that never miss.

Antistrophe
Lately from snowy Parnassus
clearly the voice flashed forth,
bidding each Theban track him down,   475
the unknown murderer.
In the savage forests he lurks and in
the caverns like
the mountain bull.
He is sad and lonely, and lonely his feet
that carry him far from the navel of earth;   480
but its prophecies, ever living,
flutter around his head.

Strophe
The augur has spread confusion,
terrible confusion;
I do not approve what was said   485
nor can I deny it.
I do not know what to say;
I am in a flutter of foreboding;
I never heard in the present
nor past of a quarrel between   490
the sons of Labdacus and Polybus,
that I might bring as proof
in attacking the popular fame
of Oedipus, seeking
to take vengeance for undiscovered
death in the line of Labdacus.   495

Antistrophe
Truly Zeus and Apollo are wise
and in human things all knowing;
but amongst men there is no   500
distinct judgment, between the prophet
and me—which of us is right.

One man may pass another in wisdom
but I would never agree
with those that find fault with the king
till I should see the word
proved right beyond doubt. For once
in visible form the Sphinx
came on him and all of us
saw his wisdom and in that test
he saved the city. So he will not be condemned by my mind.   512

(Enter Creon.)

Creon

    Citizens, I have come because I heard
deadly words spread about me, that the king
accuses me. I cannot take that from him.
If he believes that in these present troubles   515
he has been wronged by me in word or deed
I do not want to live on with the burden
of such a scandal on me. The report   520
injures me doubly and most vitally—
for I'll be called a traitor to my city
and traitor also to my friends and you.

Chorus

    Perhaps it was a sudden gust of anger
that forced that insult from him, and no judgment.

Creon

    But did he say that it was in compliance   525
with schemes of mine that the seer told him lies?

Chorus

    Yes, he said that, but why, I do not know.

Creon

    Were his eyes straight in his head? Was his mind right
when he accused me in this fashion?

Chorus

    I do not know; I have no eyes to see   530
what princes do. Here comes the king himself.

(Enter Oedipus.)

Oedipus

    You, sir, how is it you come here? Have you so much
    brazen-faced daring that you venture in
    my house although you are proved manifestly
    the murderer of that man, and though you tried,
    openly, highway robbery of my crown?   535
    For God's sake, tell me what you saw in me,
    what cowardice or what stupidity,
    that made you lay a plot like this against me?
    Did you imagine I should not observe
    the crafty scheme that stole upon me or
    seeing it, take no means to counter it?   540
    Was it not stupid of you to make the attempt,
    to try to hunt down royal power without
    the people at your back or friends? For only
    with the people at your back or money can
    the hunt end in the capture of a crown.

Creon

    Do you know what you're doing? Will you listen
    to words to answer yours, and then pass judgment?

Oedipus

    You're quick to speak, but I am slow to grasp you,   545
    for I have found you dangerous,—and my foe.

Creon

    First of all hear what I shall say to that.

Oedipus

    At least don't tell me that you are not guilty.

Creon

    If you think obstinacy without wisdom
    a valuable possession, you are wrong.   550

Oedipus

    And you are wrong if you believe that one,
    a criminal, will not be punished only
    because he is my kinsman.

Creon

This is but just—
but tell me, then, of what offense I'm guilty?

Oedipus

Did you or did you not urge me to send   555
to this prophetic mumbler?

Creon

I did indeed,
and I shall stand by what I told you.

Oedipus

How long ago is it since Laius. . . .

Creon

What about Laius? I don't understand.

Oedipus

Vanished—died—was murdered?   560

Creon

It is long,
a long, long time to reckon.

Oedipus

Was this prophet
in the profession then?

Creon

He was, and honoured
as highly as he is today.

Oedipus

At that time did he say a word about me?

Creon

Never, at least when I was near him.   565

Oedipus

You never made a search for the dead man?

Creon

We searched, indeed, but never learned of anything.

Oedipus

Why did our wise old friend not say this then?

Creon

I don't know; and when I know nothing, I
usually hold my tongue.

Oedipus

You know this much,   570
and can declare this much if you are loyal.

Creon

What is it? If I know, I'll not deny it.

Oedipus

That he would not have said that I killed Laius
had he not met you first.

Creon

You know yourself
whether he said this, but I demand that I   575
should hear as much from you as you from me.

Oedipus

Then hear,—I'll not be proved a murderer.

Creon

Well, then. You're married to my sister.

Oedipus

Yes,
that I am not disposed to deny.

Creon

You rule
this country giving her an equal share
in the government?

Oedipus

Yes, everything she wants   580
she has from me.

Creon

And I, as thirdsman to you,
am rated as the equal of you two?

Oedipus

Yes, and it's there you've proved yourself false friend.

Creon

Not if you will reflect on it as I do.
Consider, first, if you think any one
would choose to rule and fear rather than rule   585
and sleep untroubled by a fear if power
were equal in both cases. I, at least,
I was not born with such a frantic yearning
to be a king—but to do what kings do.
And so it is with every one who has learned
wisdom and self-control. As it stands now,
the prizes are all mine—and without fear.   590
But if I were the king myself, I must
do much that went against the grain.
How should despotic rule seem sweeter to me
than painless power and an assured authority?
I am not so besotted yet that I
want other honours than those that come with profit.   595
Now every man's my pleasure; every man greets me;
now those who are your suitors fawn on me,—
success for them depends upon my favour.
Why should I let all this go to win that?
My mind would not be traitor if it's wise;   600
I am no treason lover, of my nature,
nor would I ever dare to join a plot.
Prove what I say. Go to the oracle
at Pytho and inquire about the answers,
if they are as I told you. For the rest,   605
if you discover I laid any plot
together with the seer, kill me, I say,
not only by your vote but by my own.
But do not charge me on obscure opinion
without some proof to back it. It's not just
lightly to count your knaves as honest men,   610
nor honest men as knaves. To throw away
an honest friend is, as it were, to throw
your life away, which a man loves the best.

In time you will know all with certainty;
time is the only test of honest men,
one day is space enough to know a rogue.   615

Chorus

His words are wise, king, if one fears to fall.
Those who are quick of temper are not safe.

Oedipus

When he that plots against me secretly
moves quickly, I must quickly counterplot.
If I wait taking no decisive measure   620
his business will be done, and mine be spoiled.

Creon

What do you want to do then? Banish me?

Oedipus

No, certainly; kill you, not banish you.[1]

Creon

I do not think that you've your wits about you.   626

Oedipus

For my own interests, yes.

Creon

                              But for mine, too,
you should think equally.

Oedipus

                              You are a rogue.

Creon

Suppose you do not understand?

Oedipus

                              But yet
I must be ruler.

1. Two lines omitted here owing to the confusion in the dialogue consequent on
the loss of a third line. The lines as they stand in Jebb's edition (1902) are:

Oed.: That you may show what manner of thing is envy.
Creon: You speak as one that will not yield or trust.
[Oed. lost line.]

Creon

Not if you rule badly.

Oedipus

O, city, city!

Creon

I too have some share   630
in the city; it is not yours alone.

Chorus

Stop, my lords! Here—and in the nick of time
I see Jocasta coming from the house;
with her help lay the quarrel that now stirs you.

(Enter Jocasta.)

Jocasta

For shame! Why have you raised this foolish squabbling
brawl? Are you not ashamed to air your private   635
griefs when the country's sick? Go in, you, Oedipus,
and you, too, Creon, into the house. Don't magnify
your nothing troubles.

Creon

Sister, Oedipus,
your husband, thinks he has the right to do
terrible wrongs—he has but to choose between   640
two terrors: banishing or killing me.

Oedipus

He's right, Jocasta; for I find him plotting
with knavish tricks against my person.

Creon

That God may never bless me! May I die
accursed, if I have been guilty of   645
one tittle of the charge you bring against me!

Jocasta

I beg you, Oedipus, trust him in this,
spare him for the sake of this his oath to God,
for my sake, and the sake of those who stand here.

Chorus
Be gracious, be merciful,
we beg of you.   649

Oedipus
In what would you have me yield?

Chorus
He has been no silly child in the past.
He is strong in his oath now.
Spare him.

Oedipus
Do you know what you ask?

Chorus
Yes.

Oedipus
Tell me then.

Chorus

He has been your friend before all men's eyes; do not cast him   656
away dishonoured on an obscure conjecture.

Oedipus
I would have you know that this request of yours
really requests my death or banishment.

Chorus
May the Sun God, king of Gods, forbid! May I die without God's   660
blessing, without friends' help, if I had any such thought. But my
spirit is broken by my unhappiness for my wasting country; and   665
this would but add troubles amongst ourselves to the other
troubles.

Oedipus
Well, let him go then—if I must die ten times for it,   669
or be sent out dishonoured into exile.
It is your lips that prayed for him I pitied,
not his; wherever he is, I shall hate him.

Creon

    I see you sulk in yielding and you're dangerous
    when you are out of temper; natures like yours
    are justly heaviest for themselves to bear. 675

Oedipus

    Leave me alone! Take yourself off, I tell you.

Creon

    I'll go, you have not known me, but they have,
    and they have known my innocence.

                                                             (*Exit.*)

Chorus

    Won't you take him inside, lady?

Jocasta

    Yes, when I've found out what was the matter. 680

Chorus

    There was some misconceived suspicion of a story, and on the
    other side the sting of injustice.

Jocasta

    So, on both sides?

Chorus

    Yes.

Jocasta

    What was the story?

Chorus

    I think it best, in the interests of the country, to leave it where 685
    it ended.

Oedipus

    You see where you have ended, straight of judgment
    although you are, by softening my anger.

Chorus

    Sir, I have said before and I say again—be sure that I would have 689
    been proved a madman, bankrupt in sane council, if I should put
    you away, you who steered the country I love safely when she

was crazed with troubles. God grant that now, too, you may 695
prove a fortunate guide for us.

Jocasta

Tell me, my lord, I beg of you, what was it
that roused your anger so?

Oedipus

Yes, I will tell you. 700
I honour you more than I honour them.
It was Creon and the plots he laid against me.

Jocasta

Tell me—if you can clearly tell the quarrel—

Oedipus

Creon says
that I'm the murderer of Laius.

Jocasta

Of his own knowledge or on information?

Oedipus

He sent this rascal prophet to me, since 705
he keeps his own mouth clean of any guilt.

Jocasta

Do not concern yourself about this matter;
listen to me and learn that human beings
have no part in the craft of prophecy.
Of that I'll show you a short proof. 710
There was an oracle once that came to Laius,—
I will not say that it was Phoebus' own,
but it was from his servants—and it told him
that it was fate that he should die a victim
at the hands of his own son, a son to be born
of Laius and me. But, see now, he,
the king, was killed by foreign highway robbers 715
at a place where three roads meet—so goes the story;
and for the son—before three days were out
after his birth King Laius pierced his ankles

and by the hands of others cast him forth
upon a pathless hillside. So Apollo   720
failed to fulfill his oracle to the son,
that he should kill his father, and to Laius
also proved false in that the thing he feared,
death at his son's hands, never came to pass.
So clear in this case were the oracles,
so clear and false. Give them no heed, I say;
what God discovers need of, easily
he shows to us himself.   725

Oedipus
                         O dear Jocasta,
as I hear this from you, there comes upon me
a wandering of the soul—I could run mad.

Jocasta
What trouble is it, that you turn again
and speak like this?

Oedipus
                         I thought I heard you say
that Laius was killed at a crossroads.   730

Jocasta
Yes, that was how the story went and still
that word goes round.

Oedipus
                         Where is this place, Jocasta,
where he was murdered?

Jocasta
                         Phocis is the country
and the road splits there, one of two roads from Delphi,
another comes from Daulia.

Oedipus
                         How long ago is this?   735

Jocasta
The news came to the city just before

you became king and all men's eyes looked to you.
What is it, Oedipus, that's in your mind?

Oedipus
What have you designed, O Zeus, to do with me?

Jocasta
What is the thought that troubles your heart?

Oedipus
Don't ask me yet—tell me of Laius—   740
How did he look? How old or young was he?

Jocasta
He was a tall man and his hair was grizzled
already—nearly white—and in his form
not unlike you.

Oedipus
                        O God, I think I have
called curses on myself in ignorance.   745

Jocasta
What do you mean? I am terrified
when I look at you.

Oedipus
                        I have a deadly fear
that the old seer had eyes. You'll show me more
if you can tell me one more thing.

Jocasta
                        I will.
I'm frightened,—but if I can understand,
I'll tell you all you ask.

Oedipus
                        How was his company?   750
Had he few with him when he went this journey,
or many servants, as would suit a prince?

Jocasta
In all there were but five, and among them
a herald; and one carriage for the king.

Oedipus

It's plain—its plain—who was it told you this?   755

Jocasta

The only servant that escaped safe home.

Oedipus

Is he at home now?

Jocasta

No, when he came home again
and saw you king and Laius was dead,
he came to me and touched my hand and begged   760
that I should send him to the fields to be
my shepherd and so he might see the city
as far off as he might. So I
sent him away. He was an honest man,
as slaves go, and was worthy of far more
than what he asked of me.

Oedipus

O, how I wish that he could come back quickly!   765

Jocasta

He can. Why is your heart so set on this?

Oedipus

O dear Jocasta, I am full of fears
that I have spoken far too much; and therefore
I wish to see this shepherd.

Jocasta

He will come;
but, Oedipus, I think I'm worthy too
to know what it is that disquiets you.   770

Oedipus

It shall not be kept from you, since my mind
has gone so far with its forebodings. Whom
should I confide in rather than you, who is there
of more importance to me who have passed
through such a fortune?

Polybus was my father, king of Corinth,
and Merope, the Dorian, my mother.   775
I was held greatest of the citizens
in Corinth till a curious chance befell me
as I shall tell you—curious, indeed,
but hardly worth the store I set upon it.
There was a dinner and at it a man,
a drunken man, accused me in his drink   780
of being bastard. I was furious
but held my temper under for that day.
Next day I went and taxed my parents with it;
they took the insult very ill from him,
the drunken fellow who had uttered it.
So I was comforted for their part, but   785
still this thing rankled always, for the story
crept about widely. And I went at last
to Pytho, though my parents did not know.
But Phoebus sent me home again unhonoured
in what I came to learn, but he foretold   790
other and desperate horrors to befall me,
that I was fated to lie with my mother,
and show to daylight an accursed breed
which men would not endure, and I was doomed
to be murderer of the father that begot me.
When I heard this I fled, and in the days
that followed I would measure from the stars   795
the whereabouts of Corinth—yes, I fled
to somewhere where I should not see fulfilled
the infamies told in that dreadful oracle.
And as I journeyed I came to the place
where, as you say, this king met with his death.
Jocasta, I will tell you the whole truth.   800
When I was near the branching of the crossroads,
going on foot, I was encountered by
a herald and a carriage with a man in it,
just as you tell me. He that led the way

and the old man himself wanted to thrust me 805
out of the road by force. I became angry
and struck the coachman who was pushing me.
When the old man saw this he watched his moment,
and as I passed he struck me from his carriage,
full on the head with his two pointed goad.
But he was paid in full and presently 810
my stick had struck him backwards from the car
and he rolled out of it. And then I killed them
all. If it happened there was any tie
of kinship twixt this man and Laius,
who is then now more miserable than I, 815
what man on earth so hated by the Gods,
since neither citizen nor foreigner
may welcome me at home or even greet me,
but drive me out of doors? And it is I,
I and no other have so cursed myself. 820
And I pollute the bed of him I killed
by the hands that killed him. Was I not born evil?
Am I not utterly unclean? I had to fly
and in my banishment not even see
my kindred nor set foot in my own country,
or otherwise my fate was to be yoked 825
in marriage with my mother and kill my father,
Polybus who begot me and had reared me.
Would not one rightly judge and say that on me
these things were sent by some malignant God?
O no, no, no—O holy majesty 830
of God on high, may I not see that day!
May I be gone out of men's sight before
I see the deadly taint of this disaster
come upon me.

Chorus

Sir, we too fear these things. But until you see this man face to
face and hear his story, hope. 835

Oedipus

Yes, I have just this much of hope—to wait until the herdsman comes.

Jocasta

And when he comes, what do you want with him?

Oedipus

I'll tell you; if I find that his story is the same as yours, I at least will be clear of this guilt.   840

Jocasta

Why what so particularly did you learn from my story?

Oedipus

You said that he spoke of highway *robbers* who killed Laius. Now if he uses the same number, it was not I who killed him. One man cannot be the same as many. But if he speaks of a man travelling   845 alone, then clearly the burden of the guilt inclines towards me.

Jocasta

Be sure, at least, that this was how he told the story. He cannot unsay it now, for every one in the city heard it—not I alone. But,   850 Oedipus, even if he diverges from what he said then, he shall never prove that the murder of Laius squares rightly with the prophecy—for Loxias declared that the king should be killed by his own son. And that poor creature did not kill him surely,—   855 for he died himself first. So as far as prophecy goes, henceforward I shall not look to the right hand or the left.

Oedipus

Right. But yet, send some one for the peasant to bring him here;   860 do not neglect it.

Jocasta

I will send quickly. Now let me go indoors. I will do nothing except what pleases you.

(*Exeunt.*)

Chorus

  Strophe

May destiny ever find me

pious in word and deed   865
prescribed by the laws that live on high:
laws begotten in the clear air of heaven,
whose only father is Olympus;
no mortal nature brought them to birth,
no forgetfulness shall lull them to sleep;   870
for God is great in them and grows not old.

Antistrophe
Insolence breeds the tyrant, insolence
if it is glutted with a surfeit, unseasonable, unprofitable,   875
climbs to the roof-top and plunges
sheer down to the ruin that must be,
and there its feet are no service.
But I pray that the God may never   880
abolish the eager ambition that profits the state.
For I shall never cease to hold the God as our protector.

Strophe
If a man walks with haughtiness
of hand or word and gives no heed   885
to Justice and the shrines of Gods
despises—may an evil doom
smite him for his ill-starred pride of heart!—
if he reaps gains without justice
and will not hold from impiety   890
and his fingers itch for untouchable things.
When such things are done, what man shall contrive
to shield his soul from the shafts of the God?
When such deeds are held in honour,   895
why should I honour the Gods in the dance?

Antistrophe
No longer to the holy place,
to the navel of earth I'll go
to worship, nor to Abae
nor to Olympia,   900
unless the oracles are proved to fit,
for all men's hands to point at.

O Zeus, if you are rightly called
the sovereign lord, all-mastering,
let this not escape you nor your ever-living power!   905
The oracles concerning Laius
are old and dim and men regard them not.
Apollo is nowhere clear in honour; God's service perishes.   910

(Enter Jocasta, carrying garlands.)

Jocasta

Princes of the land, I have had the thought to go
to the Gods' temples, bringing in my hand
garlands and gifts of incense, as you see.
For Oedipus excites himself too much
at every sort of trouble, not conjecturing,   915
like a man of sense, what will be from what was,
but he is always at the speaker's mercy,
when he speaks terrors. I can do no good
by my advice, and so I came as suppliant
to you, Lycaean Apollo, who are nearest.
These are the symbols of my prayer and this   920
my prayer: grant us escape free of the curse.
Now when we look to him we are all afraid;
he's pilot of our ship and he is frightened.

(Enter Messenger.)

Messenger

Might I learn from you, sirs, where is the house of Oedipus? Or   925
best of all, if you know, where is the king himself?

Chorus

This is his house and he is within doors. This lady is his wife and
mother of his children.

Messenger

God bless you, lady, and God bless your household! God bless   930
Oedipus' noble wife!

Jocasta

God bless you, sir, for your kind greeting! What do you want
of us that you have come here? What have you to tell us?

Messenger

Good news, lady. Good for your house and for your husband.

Jocasta

What is your news? Who sent you to us?   935

Messenger

I come from Corinth and the news I bring will give you pleasure.
Perhaps a little pain too.

Jocasta

What is this news of double meaning?

Messenger

The people of the Isthmus will choose Oedipus to be their king.   940
That is the rumour there.

Jocasta

But isn't their king still old Polybus?

Messenger

No. He is in his grave. Death has got him.

Jocasta

Is that the truth? Is Oedipus' father dead?

Messenger

May I die myself if it be otherwise!

Jocasta (to a servant)

Be quick and run to the King with the news! O oracles of the   945
Gods, where are you now? It was from this man Oedipus fled, lest
he should be his murderer! And now he is dead, in the course of
nature, and not killed by Oedipus.

(Enter Oedipus.)

Oedipus

Dearest Jocasta, why have you sent for me?   950

Jocasta

Listen to this man and when you hear reflect what is the outcome
of the holy oracles of the Gods.

Oedipus

Who is he? What is his message for me?

Jocasta

He is from Corinth and he tells us that your father Polybus is   955
dead and gone.

Oedipus

What's this you say, sir? Tell me yourself.

Messenger

Since this is the first matter you want clearly told: Polybus has
gone down to death. You may be sure of it.

Oedipus

By treachery or sickness?   960

Messenger

A small thing will put old bodies asleep.

Oedipus

So he died of sickness, it seems,—poor old man!

Messenger

Yes, and of age—the long years he had measured.

Oedipus

Ha! Ha! O dear Jocasta, why should one
look to the Pythian hearth? Why should one look   965
to the birds screaming overhead? They prophesied
that I should kill my father! But he's dead,
and hidden deep in earth, and I stand here
who never laid a hand on spear against him,—
unless perhaps he died of longing for me,
and thus I am his murderer. But they,   970
the oracles, as they stand—he's taken them
away with him, they're dead as he himself is,
and worthless.

Jocasta

                        That I told you before now.

Oedipus

You did, but I was misled by my fear.

Jocasta

Then lay no more of them to heart, not one   975

Oedipus
> But surely I must fear my mother's bed?

Jocasta
> Why should man fear since chance is all in all
> for him, and he can clearly foreknow nothing?
> Best to live lightly, as one can, unthinkingly.
> As to your mother's marriage bed,—don't fear it.   980
> Before this, in dreams too, as well as oracles,
> many a man has lain with his own mother.
> But he to whom such things are nothing bears
> his life most easily.

Oedipus
> All that you say would be said perfectly
> if she were dead; but since she lives I must   985
> still fear, although you talk so well, Jocasta.

Jocasta
> Still in your father's death there's light of comfort?

Oedipus
> Great light of comfort; but I fear the living.

Messenger
> Who is the woman that makes you afraid?

Oedipus
> Merope, old man, Polybus' wife.   990

Messenger
> What about her frightens the queen and you?

Oedipus
> A terrible oracle, stranger, from the Gods.

Messenger
> Can it be told? Or does the sacred law
> forbid another to have knowledge of it?

Oedipus
> O no! Once on a time Loxias said
> that I should lie with my own mother and   995

take on my hands the blood of my own father.
And so for these long years I've lived away
from Corinth; it has been to my great happiness;
but yet it's sweet to see the face of parents.

Messenger
This was the fear which drove you out of Corinth?   1000

Oedipus
Old man, I did not wish to kill my father.

Messenger
Why should I not free you from this fear, sir,
since I have come to you in all goodwill?

Oedipus
You would not find me thankless if you did.

Messenger
Why, it was just for this I brought the news,—   1005
to earn your thanks when you had come safe home.

Oedipus
No, I will never come near my parents.

Messenger
                    Son,
it's very plain you don't know what you're doing.

Oedipus
What do you mean, old man? For God's sake, tell me.

Messenger
If your homecoming is checked by fears like these.   1010

Oedipus
Yes, I'm afraid that Phoebus may prove right.

Messenger
The murder and the incest?

Oedipus
                    Yes, old man;
that is my constant terror.

Messenger
                        Do you know
that all your fears are empty?

Oedipus
                        How is that,   1015
if they are father and mother and I their son?

Messenger
Because Polybus was no kin to you in blood.

Oedipus
What, was not Polybus my father?

Messenger
No more than I but just so much.

Oedipus
                        How can
my father be my father as much as one
that's nothing to me?

Messenger
                        Neither he nor I   1020
begat you.

Oedipus
                        Why then did he call me son?

Messenger
A gift he took you from these hands of mine.

Oedipus
Did he love so much what he took from another's hand?

Messenger
His childlessness before persuaded him.

Oedipus
Was I a child you bought or found when I   1025
was given to him?

Messenger
                        On Cithaeron's slopes
in the twisting thickets you were found.

Oedipus
>   And why
>   were you a traveller in those parts?

Messenger
>   I was
>   in charge of mountain flocks.

Oedipus
>   You were a shepherd?
>   A hireling vagrant?

Messenger
>   Yes, but at least at that time   1030
>   the man that saved your life, son.

Oedipus
>   What ailed me when you took me in your arms?

Messenger
>   In that your ankles should be witnesses.

Oedipus
>   Why do you speak of that old pain?

Messenger
>   I loosed you;
>   the tendons of your feet were pierced and fettered,—

Oedipus
>   My swaddling clothes brought me a rare disgrace.   1035

Messenger
>   So that from this you're called your present name.

Oedipus
>   Was this my father's doing or my mother's?
>   For God's sake, tell me.

Messenger
>   I don't know, but he
>   who gave you to me has more knowledge than I.

Oedipus
>   You yourself did not find me then? You took me
>   from someone else?

Messenger

Yes, from another shepherd.   1040

Oedipus

Who was he? Do you know him well enough
to tell?

Messenger

He was called Laius' man.

Oedipus

You mean the king who reigned here in the old days?

Messenger

Yes, he was that man's shepherd.

Oedipus

Is he alive   1045
still, so that I could see him?

Messenger

You who live here
would know that best.

Oedipus

Do any of you here
know of this shepherd whom he speaks about
in town or in the fields? Tell me. It's time   1050
that this was found out once for all.

Chorus

I think he is none other than the peasant
whom you have sought to see already; but
Jocasta here can tell us best of that.

Oedipus

Jocasta, do you know about this man
whom we have sent for? Is he the man he mentions?   1055

Jocasta

Why ask of whom he spoke? Don't give it heed;
nor try to keep in mind what has been said.
It will be wasted labour.

Oedipus
>   With such clues
> I could not fail to bring my birth to light.

Jocasta
> I beg you—do not hunt this out—I beg you,   1060
> if you have any care for your own life.
> What I am suffering is enough.

Oedipus
>   Keep up
> your heart, Jocasta. Though I'm proved a slave,
> thrice slave, and though my mother is thrice slave,
> you'll not be shown to be of lowly lineage.

Jocasta
> O be persuaded by me, I entreat you;
> do not do this.

Oedipus
> I will not be persuaded to let be   1065
> the chance of finding out the whole thing clearly.

Jocasta
> It is because I wish you well that I
> give you this counsel—and it's the best counsel.

Oedipus
> Then the best counsel vexes me, and has
> for some while since.

Jocasta
>   O Oedipus, God help you!
> God keep you from the knowledge of who you are!

Oedipus
> Here, some one, go and fetch the shepherd for me;
> and let her find her joy in her rich family!   1070

Jocasta
> O Oedipus, unhappy Oedipus!
> that is all I can call you, and the last thing
> that I shall ever call you.
>
>   (*Exit.*)

Chorus

    Why has the queen gone, Oedipus, in wild
    grief rushing from us? I am afraid that trouble   1075
    will break out of this silence.

Oedipus

    Break out what will! I at least shall be
    willing to see my ancestry, though humble.
    Perhaps she is ashamed of my low birth,
    for she has all a woman's high-flown pride.
    But I account myself a child of Fortune,   1080
    beneficent Fortune, and I shall not be
    dishonoured. She's the mother from whom I spring;
    the months, my brothers, marked me, now as small,
    and now again as mighty. Such is my breeding,
    and I shall never prove so false to it,   1085
    as not to find the secret of my birth.

Chorus

    Strophe

    If I am a prophet and wise of heart
    you shall not fail, Cithaeron,   1090
    by the limitless sky, you shall not!—
    to know at tomorrow's full moon
    that Oedipus honours you,
    as native to him and mother and nurse at once;
    and that you are honoured in dancing by us, as finding favour in
        sight of our king.
    Apollo, to whom we cry, find these things pleasing!

    Antistrophe

    Who was it bore you, child? One of   1098
    the long-lived nymphs who lay with Pan—
    the father who treads the hills?
    Or was she a bride of Loxias, your mother? The grassy slopes
    are all of them dear to him. Or perhaps Cyllene's king   1104
    or the Bacchants' God that lives on the tops

of the hills received you a gift from some
one of the Helicon Nymphs, with whom he mostly plays?

(*Enter an old man, led by Oedipus' servants.*)

Oedipus

If some one like myself who never met him   1110
may make a guess,—I think this is the herdsman,
whom we were seeking. His old age is consonant
with the other. And besides, the men who bring him
I recognize as my own servants. You   1115
perhaps may better me in knowledge since
you've seen the man before.

Chorus

You can be sure
I recognize him. For if Laius
had ever an honest shepherd, this was he.

Oedipus

You, sir, from Corinth, I must ask you first,
is this the man you spoke of?   1120

Messenger

This is he
before your eyes.

Oedipus

Old man, look here at me
and tell me what I ask you. Were you ever
a servant of King Laius?

Herdsman

I was,—
no slave he bought but reared in his own house.

Oedipus

What did you do as work? How did you live?

Herdsman

Most of my life was spent among the flocks.   1125

Oedipus

In what part of the country did you live?

Herdsman

Cithaeron and the places near to it.

Oedipus

And somewhere there perhaps you knew this man?

Herdsman

What was his occupation? Who?

Oedipus

                This man here,   1130
have you had any dealings with him?

Herdsman

            No—
not such that I can quickly call to mind.

Messenger

That is no wonder, master. But I'll make him remember what he
does not know. For I know, that he well knows the country of
Cithaeron, how he with two flocks, I with one kept company for   1135
three years—each year half a year—from spring till autumn time
and then when winter came I drove my flocks to our fold home
again and he to Laius' steadings. Well—am I right or not in what   1140
I said we did?

Herdsman

You're right—although it's a long time ago.

Messenger

Do you remember giving me a child
to bring up as my foster child?

Herdsman

              What's this?
Why do you ask this question?

Messenger

             Look old man,   1145
here he is—here's the man who was that child!

Herdsman

Death take you! Won't you hold your tongue?

Oedipus
                              No, no,
   do not find fault with him, old man. Your words
   are more at fault than his.

Herdsman
                              O best of masters,
   how do I give offense?

Oedipus
                              When you refuse   1150
   to speak about the child of whom he asks you.

Herdsman
   He speaks out of his ignorance, without meaning.

Oedipus
   If you'll not talk to gratify me, you
   will talk with pain to urge you.

Herdsman
                              O please, sir,
   don't hurt an old man, sir.

Oedipus (to the servants)
                              Here, one of you,
   twist his hands behind him.

Herdsman
                              Why, God help me, why?   1155
   What do you want to know?

Oedipus
                              You gave a child
   to him,—the child he asked you of?

Herdsman
                              I did.
   I wish I'd died the day I did.

Oedipus
                              You will
   unless you tell me truly.

Herdsman

And I'll die
far worse if I should tell you.

Oedipus

This fellow   1160
is bent on more delays, as it would seem.

Herdsman

O no, no! I have told you that I gave it.

Oedipus

Where did you get this child from? Was it your own or did you
get it from another?

Herdsman

Not
my own at all; I had it from some one.

Oedipus

One of these citizens? or from what house?

Herdsman

O master, please—I beg you, master, please   1165
don't ask me more.

Oedipus

You're a dead man if I
ask you again.

Herdsman

It was one of the children
of Laius.

Oedipus

A slave? Or born in wedlock?

Herdsman

O God, I am on the brink of frightful speech.

Oedipus

And I of frightful hearing. But I must hear.   1170

Herdsman

The child was called his child; but she within,
your wife would tell you best how all this was.

Oedipus

She gave it to you?

Herdsman

Yes, she did, my lord.

Oedipus

To do what with it?

Herdsman

Make away with it.

Oedipus

She was so hard—its mother?   1175

Herdsman

Aye, through fear

of evil oracles.

Oedipus

Which?

Herdsman

They said that he

should kill his parents.

Oedipus

How was it that you

gave it away to this old man?

Herdsman

O master,

I pitied it, and thought that I could send it

off to another country and this man

was from another country. But he saved it   1180

for the most terrible troubles. If you are

the man he says you are, you're bred to misery.

Oedipus

O, O, O, they will all come,

all come out clearly! Light of the sun, let me

look upon you no more after today!

I who first saw the light bred of a match

accursed, and accursed in my living

with them I lived with, cursed in my killing.   1185

(*Exeunt all but the Chorus.*)

« 63 »

Chorus

Strophe

O generations of men, how I
count you as equal with those who live
not at all!
What man, what man on earth wins more   1190
of happiness than a seeming
and after that turning away?
Oedipus, you are my pattern of this,
Oedipus, you and your fate!
Luckless Oedipus, whom of all men
I envy not at all.   1196

Antistrophe

In as much as he shot his bolt
beyond the others and won the prize
of happiness complete—
O Zeus—and killed and reduced to nought
the hooked taloned maid of the riddling speech,
standing a tower against death for my land:
hence he was called my king and hence
was honoured the highest of all
honours; and hence he ruled
in the great city of Thebes.

Strophe

But now whose tale is more miserable?   1204
Who is there lives with a savager fate?
Whose troubles so reverse his life as his?

O Oedipus, the famous prince
for whom a great haven
the same both as father and son
sufficed for generation,
how, O how, have the furrows ploughed
by your father endured to bear you, poor wretch,
and hold their peace so long?

Antistrophe

Time who sees all has found you out   1213
against your will; judges your marriage accursed,
begetter and begot at one in it.

O child of Laius,
would I had never seen you.
I weep for you and cry
a dirge of lamentation.

To speak directly, I drew my breath
from you at the first and so now I lull   1222
my mouth to sleep with your name.

                    (*Enter a second messenger.*)

Second Messenger

O Princes always honoured by our country,
what deeds you'll hear of and what horrors see,
what grief you'll feel, if you as true born Thebans   1225
care for the house of Labdacus's sons.
Phasis nor Ister cannot purge this house,
I think, with all their streams, such things
it hides, such evils shortly will bring forth
into the light, whether they will or not;   1230
and troubles hurt the most
when they prove self-inflicted.

Chorus

What we had known before did not fall short
of bitter groaning's worth; what's more to tell?

Second Messenger

Shortest to hear and tell—our glorious queen   1235
Jocasta's dead.

Chorus

                    Unhappy woman! How?

Second Messenger

By her own hand. The worst of what was done
you cannot know. You did not see the sight.
Yet in so far as I remember it

you'll hear the end of our unlucky queen.   1240
When she came raging into the house she went
straight to her marriage bed, tearing her hair
with both her hands, and crying upon Laius   1245
long dead—Do you remember, Laius,
that night long past which bred a child for us
to send you to your death and leave
a mother making children with her son?
And then she groaned and cursed the bed in which
she brought forth husband by her husband, children   1250
by her own child, an infamous double bond.
How after that she died I do not know,—
for Oedipus distracted us from seeing.
He burst upon us shouting and we looked
to him as he paced frantically around,
begging us always: Give me a sword, I say,   1255
to find this wife no wife, this mother's womb,
this field of double sowing whence I sprang
and where I sowed my children! As he raved
some god showed him the way—none of us there.
Bellowing terribly and led by some   1260
invisible guide he rushed on the two doors,—
wrenching the hollow bolts out of their sockets,
he charged inside. There, there, we saw his wife
hanging, the twisted rope around her neck.
When he saw her, he cried out fearfully   1265
and cut the dangling noose. Then, as she lay,
poor woman, on the ground, what happened after,
was terrible to see. He tore the brooches—
the gold chased brooches fastening her robe—
away from her and lifting them up high
dashed them on his own eyeballs, shrieking out   1270
such things as: they will never see the crime
I have committed or had done upon me!
Dark eyes, now in the days to come look on
forbidden faces, do not recognize

those whom you long for—with such imprecations
he struck his eyes again and yet again   1275
with the brooches. And the bleeding eyeballs gushed
and stained his beard—no sluggish oozing drops
but a black rain and bloody hail poured down.

So it has broken—and not on one head   1280
but troubles mixed for husband and for wife.
The fortune of the days gone by was true
good fortune—but today groans and destruction
and death and shame—of all ills can be named   1285
not one is missing.

Chorus
    Is he now in any ease from pain?

Second Messenger
                He shouts
for some one to unbar the doors and show him
to all the men of Thebes, his father's killer,
his mother's—no I cannot say the word,
it is unholy—for he'll cast himself,
out of the land, he says, and not remain   1290
to bring a curse upon his house, the curse
he called upon it in his proclamation. But
he wants for strength, aye, and some one to guide him;
his sickness is too great to bear. You, too,
will be shown that. The bolts are opening.   1295
Soon you will see a sight to waken pity
even in the horror of it.

                    (Enter the blinded Oedipus.)

Chorus
    This is a terrible sight for men to see!
    I never found a worse!
    Poor wretch, what madness came upon you!   1300
    What evil spirit leaped upon your life
    to your ill-luck—a leap beyond man's strength!
    Indeed I pity you, but I cannot

look at you, though there's much I want to ask
and much to learn and much to see.   1305
I shudder at the sight of you.

Oedipus

O, O,
where am I going? Where is my voice   1310
borne on the wind to and fro?
Spirit, how far have you sprung?

Chorus

To a terrible place whereof men's ears
may not hear, nor their eyes behold it.

Oedipus

Darkness!
Horror of darkness enfolding, resistless, unspeakable visitant sped
    by an ill wind in haste!   1315
madness and stabbing pain and memory
of evil deeds I have done!

Chorus

In such misfortunes it's no wonder
if double weighs the burden of your grief.   1320

Oedipus

My friend,
you are the only one steadfast, the only one that attends on me;
you still stay nursing the blind man.
Your care is not unnoticed. I can know   1325
your voice, although this darkness is my world.

Chorus

Doer of dreadful deeds, how did you dare
so far to do despite to your own eyes?
what spirit urged you to it?

Oedipus

It was Apollo, friends, Apollo,
that brought this bitter bitterness, my sorrows to completion.   1330
But the hand that struck me

was none but my own.
Why should I see
whose vision showed me nothing sweet to see? 1335

Chorus
These things are as you say.

Oedipus
What can I see to love?
What greeting can touch my ears with joy?
Take me away, and haste—to a place out of the way! 1340
Take me away, my friends, the greatly miserable,
the most accursed, whom God too hates 1345
above all men on earth!

Chorus
Unhappy in your mind and your misfortune,
would I had never known you!

Oedipus
Curse on the man who took
the cruel bonds from off my legs, as I lay in the field. 1350
He stole me from death and saved me,
no kindly service.
Had I died then
I would not be so burdensome to friends. 1355

Chorus
I, too, could have wished it had been so.

Oedipus
Then I would not have come
to kill my father and marry my mother infamously.
Now I am godless and child of impurity, 1360
begetter in the same seed that created my wretched self.
If there is any ill worse than ill, 1365
that is the lot of Oedipus.

Chorus
I cannot say your remedy was good;
you would be better dead than blind and living.

Oedipus

What I have done here was best done—don't tell me 1370
otherwise, do not give me further counsel.
I do not know with what eyes I could look
upon my father when I die and go
under the earth, nor yet my wretched mother—
those two to whom I have done things deserving
worse punishment than hanging. Would the sight 1375
of children, bred as mine are, gladden me?
No, not these eyes, never. And my city,
its towers and sacred places of the Gods,
of these I robbed my miserable self 1380
when I commanded all to drive *him* out,
the criminal since proved by God impure
and of the race of Laius.
To this guilt I bore witness against myself—
with what eyes shall I look upon my people? 1385
No. If there were a means to choke the fountain
of hearing I would not have stayed my hand
from locking up my miserable carcase,
seeing and hearing nothing; it is sweet 1390
to keep our thoughts out of the range of hurt.

Cithaeron, why did you receive me? why
having received me did you not kill me straight?
And so I had not shown to men my birth.

O Polybus and Corinth and the house,
the old house that I used to call my father's— 1395
what fairness you were nurse to, and what foulness
festered beneath! Now I am found to be
a sinner and a son of sinners. Crossroads,
and hidden glade, oak and the narrow way
at the crossroads, that drank my father's blood 1400
offered you by my hands, do you remember
still what I did as you looked on, and what
I did when I came here? O marriage, marriage!

you bred me and again when you had bred
bred children of your child and showed to men   1405
brides, wives and mothers and the foulest deeds
that can be in this world of ours.

Come—it's unfit to say what is unfit
to do.—I beg of you in God's name hide me   1410
somewhere outside your country, yes, or kill me,
or throw me into the sea, to be forever
out of your sight. Approach and deign to touch me
for all my wretchedness, and do not fear.
No man but I can bear my evil doom.   1415

Chorus

Here Creon comes in fit time to perform
or give advice in what you ask of us.
Creon is left sole ruler in your stead.

Oedipus

Creon! Creon! What shall I say to him?
How can I justly hope that he will trust me?   1420
In what is past I have been proved towards him
an utter liar.

                                        (*Enter Creon.*)

Creon

                        Oedipus, I've come
not so that I might laugh at you nor taunt you
with evil of the past. But if you still
are without shame before the face of men
reverence at least the flame that gives all life,   1425
our Lord the Sun, and do not show unveiled
to him pollution such that neither land
nor holy rain nor light of day can welcome.

                                        (*To a servant.*)

Be quick and take him in. It is most decent   1430
that only kin should see and hear the troubles
of kin.

« 71 »

Oedipus

I beg you, since you've torn me from
my dreadful expectations and have come
in a most noble spirit to a man
that has used you vilely—do a thing for me.
I shall speak for your own good, not for my own.

Creon

What do you need that you would ask of me?   1435

Oedipus

Drive me from here with all the speed you can
to where I may not hear a human voice.

Creon

Be sure, I would have done this had not I
wished first of all to learn from the God the course
of action I should follow.

Oedipus

But his word   1440
has been quite clear to let the parricide,
the sinner, die.

Creon

Yes, that indeed was said.
But in the present need we had best discover
what we should do.

Oedipus

And will you ask about
a man so wretched?

Creon

Now even you will trust   1445
the God.

Oedipus

So. I command you—and will beseech you—
to her that lies inside that house give burial
as you would have it; she is yours and rightly
you will perform the rites for her. For me—

never let this my father's city have me   1450
living a dweller in it. Leave me live
in the mountains where Cithaeron is, that's called
my mountain, which my mother and my father
while they were living would have made my tomb.
So I may die by their decree who sought
indeed to kill me. Yet I know this much: 1455
no sickness and no other thing will kill me.
I would not have been saved from death if not
for some strange evil fate. Well, let my fate
go where it will.

      Creon, you need not care   1460
about my sons; they're men and so wherever
they are, they will not lack a livelihood.
But my two girls—so sad and pitiful—
whose table never stood apart from mine,
and everything I touched they always shared—   1465
O Creon, have a thought for them! And most
I wish that you might suffer me to touch them
and sorrow with them.

    (*Enter Antigone and Ismene, Oedipus' two daughters.*)
O my lord! O true noble Creon! Can I   1470
really be touching them, as when I saw?
What shall I say?
Yes, I can hear them sobbing—my two darlings!
and Creon has had pity and has sent me
what I loved most?
Am I right?   1475

Creon

  You're right: it was I gave you this
because I knew from old days how you loved them
as I see now.

Oedipus

      God bless you for it, Creon,
and may God guard you better on your road
than he did me!

O children,   1480
where are you? Come here, come to my hands,
a brother's hands which turned your father's eyes,
those bright eyes you knew once, to what you see,
a father seeing nothing, knowing nothing,
begetting you from his own source of life.   1485
I weep for you—I cannot see your faces—
I weep when I think of the bitterness
there will be in your lives, how you must live
before the world. At what assemblages
of citizens will you make one? to what   1490
gay company will you go and not come home
in tears instead of sharing in the holiday?
And when you're ripe for marriage, who will he be,
the man who'll risk to take such infamy
as shall cling to my children, to bring hurt   1495
on them and those that marry with them? What
curse is not there? "Your father killed his father
and sowed the seed where he had sprung himself
and begot you out of the womb that held him."
These insults you will hear. Then who will marry you?   1500
No one, my children; clearly you are doomed
to waste away in barrenness unmarried.
Son of Menoeceus, since you are all the father
left these two girls, and we, their parents, both   1505
are dead to them—do not allow them wander
like beggars, poor and husbandless.
They are of your own blood.
And do not make them equal with myself
in wretchedness; for you can see them now
so young, so utterly alone, save for you only.
Touch my hand, noble Creon, and say yes.   1510
If you were older, children, and were wiser,
there's much advice I'd give you. But as it is,
let this be what you pray: give me a life

wherever there is opportunity
to live, and better life than was my father's.

Creon

Your tears have had enough of scope; now go within the house.   1515

Oedipus

I must obey, though bitter of heart.

Creon

In season, all is good.

Oedipus

Do you know on what conditions I obey?

Creon

                    You tell me them,
and I shall know them when I hear.

Oedipus

                    That you shall send me out
to live away from Thebes.

Creon

            That gift you must ask of the God.

Oedipus

But I'm now hated by the Gods.

Creon

            So quickly you'll obtain your prayer.

Oedipus

You consent then?   1520

Creon

            What I do not mean, I do not use to say.

Oedipus

Now lead me away from here.

Creon

            Let go the children, then, and come.

Oedipus

Do not take them from me.

Creon

        Do not seek to be master in everything,
for the things you mastered did not follow you throughout your
   life.

                 (*As Creon and Oedipus go out.*)

Chorus

You that live in my ancestral Thebes, behold this Oedipus,—
him who knew the famous riddles and was a man most masterful;   1525
not a citizen who did not look with envy on his lot—
see him now and see the breakers of misfortune swallow him!
Look upon that last day always. Count no mortal happy till
he has passed the final limit of his life secure from pain.   1530